To Rachel

Thanks
as YF—
and lov
for colle

God bless

Lorna,

Gareth

Maura.

Alastair.

Richard

Gillian

Michelle

lots & Love
Tracey x.

Margaret

Janet.

Sarech
xx

Thomas /xxx.

THE
POCKET OXFORD
BOOK OF
PRAYER

THE
POCKET OXFORD
BOOK OF
PRAYER

—

GENERAL EDITOR
GEORGE APPLETON

OXFORD UNIVERSITY PRESS
1989

Oxford University Press, Walton Street, Oxford OX2 6DP

Oxford New York Toronto
Delhi Bombay Calcutta Madras Karachi
Petaling Jaya Singapore Hong Kong Tokyo
Nairobi Dar es Salaam Cape Town
Melbourne Auckland

and associated companies in
Berlin Ibadan

Oxford is a trade mark of Oxford University Press

First published 1989

British Library Cataloguing in Publication Data
The Pocket Oxford book of prayer
1. Prayers
I. Appleton, George, 1902–
291.43

ISBN 0-19-122441-3

Printed in
Great Britain
by Anchor Press Ltd.
Tiptree, Essex

Contents

	Introduction	vii
1.	Preparing to Pray	1
2.	Prayers of Worship	7
3.	Forgiveness and Penitence	21
4.	The Lord's Prayer	29
5.	The Eucharist	43
6.	Listening to God	51
7.	Praying for the World	61
8.	Praying for the Church	75
9.	How Others Pray	83
10.	Prayers of Devotion	93
11.	The Beyond	103
12.	Final Blessings	109
	Acknowledgements	113

Introduction

It is a great joy to hear from different parts of the world that the Oxford Book of Prayer is proving so helpful. It is also a matter of satisfaction that a paperback edition has been produced, beautifully printed, and published at an amazingly low price, which will enable many more people to enjoy and use it. I welcomed the suggestion from the liturgical editor of Oxford University Press that a pocket edition should be published, and am glad to have assisted in this third development of the original project. I hope that *The Pocket Oxford Book of Prayer* will inspire busy people in their own personal devotions.

To make a choice of something over 100 prayers out of 1,100 is not an easy task, for there are so many more that I value and use regularly. This is therefore a very personal selection. The preparation of the book took much longer than I anticipated, for I found myself caught up in the original praying and the words in which each prayer was expressed. Any other of the original editorial group could produce an equally personal and good selection, which would represent the essence of our joint effort.

There are several addenda, recognizing new needs and timely prayers, which we hope will help create the spiritual atmosphere in which God's grace and blessing may be outpoured on our troubled world,

and his righteous and loving will may be perceived
and obeyed.

G.A.

Michaelmas 1988

I

PREPARING TO PRAY

1. PREPARING TO PRAY

In our earliest practice of prayer, either as children or as not yet mature and spiritual persons, many of us were content with saying prayers. We probably began our speaking to God without realizing his presence, without giving Him our full attention and laying aside the immediate concerns that had been occupying our attention. Nor did we appreciate fully the amazing privilege of entering into personal relationship with the Creator of all, who comes to each one of us, who loves each one and all of us simultaneously, holding each one of us and all of us in his all-embracing heart. Words, however eloquent, cannot fully express the wonder of his Being, his never failing love, his inexhaustible grace.

Our preparation for prayer is an essential part of prayer, opening the heart to Him, focusing our attention on Him, enjoying Him, trusting Him, expressing our need of Him, loving Him, wanted to be like Him, wanting his guidance and supporting grace in the happenings of life, its duties, difficulties, opportunities, and adventures.

We may need some help in getting going, in

tuning in to the spiritual wavelength, even some words which can be slowly repeated, until they lead us into silent stillness and consciousness of his presence. Vocal prayer needs to be punctuated by stillness. The following short verses have helped and inspired seekers and finders of God all down the ages since people began to suspect, hope, and realize that in the deeps of their being they were more than just physical, more than just temporary, wonderfully created by the Eternal Spirit and to enter into his eternity and love.

Stilling the mind

Be still then and know that I am God. *Ps. 46: 10*

God Thou art my God, early will I seek Thee.
Ps. 63: 1

My soul is athirst for God, yea, even for the living God. *Ps. 42: 2*

Love for God

I will love Thee, O Lord my strength; the Lord is my rock and my defence; my Saviour, my God and my might. *Ps. 18: 1*

Abba, Father. Father, dear Father. *Mark 14: 36*

Lord, Thou knowest all things; Thou knowest that I love Thee. *John 21: 17*

Our chiefest good

I have said unto the Lord, 'Thou art my God. I have no good beyond Thee.' *Ps. 16: 2 R.V.*

And now, Lord, what is my hope: truly my hope is in Thee. *Ps. 39: 7*

Though I am sometimes afraid, yet put I my trust in Thee. *Ps. 56: 3*

Our need for God

Lord, give me this water, that I thirst not again. *John 4: 15*

Lord, give us this bread always. *John 6: 34*

Lord, to whom (*else*) shall we go? You have the words of eternal life. *John 6: 68*

Guidance for life

Thou shalt show me the path of life. *Ps. 16: 11*

Lord, what wilt Thou have me to do? *Acts 9: 6*

Show Thou me the way that I should walk in, for I lift up my heart to Thee. *Ps. 143: 5b*

4

Strength for life

I can do all things in Him who strengthens me.

Phil. 4: 13

My strength is made perfect in weakness.

2 Cor. 12: 9

Nothing can separate us from the love of God in
Christ Jesus, our Lord. *Romans 8: 39*

Last thing at night

Stay with us, for it is towards evening and the
day is far spent. *Luke 24: 29*

Preserve us, O Lord, while waking, and guard
us while sleeping, that awake we may watch
with Christ, and asleep we may rest in peace.

Compline Prayer

Night is drawing nigh
For all that has been—Thanks!
For all that shall be—Yes! *Dag Hammarskjöld*

The grace of the Lord Jesus Christ, and the love
of God, and the fellowship of the Holy Spirit
be with you all. *2 Cor. 13: 14*

Towards the end

Even to old age, I am He, and to gray hairs I will carry you, I have made, and I will bear.

Isaiah 46: 4

You have kept the good wine until now.

John 2: 10

Father, into thy hands I commend my spirit.

Luke 23: 46

It is I, be not afraid.

Matthew 14: 27

2

PRAYERS OF WORSHIP

2. PRAYERS OF WORSHIP

Worship is the submission of all our nature
to God. It is the quickening of conscience by
his holiness; the nourishment of mind with
his truth; the purifying of the imagination
by his beauty; the opening of the heart to his
love; the surrender of will to his purpose—
and all of this gathered up in adoration, the
most selfless emotion of which our nature is
capable and therefore the chief remedy of that
self-centredness which is our original sin and
the source of all actual sin.

William Temple, 1881–1944

To adore . . That means to lose oneself in the
unfathomable, to plunge into the inexhaustible,
to find peace in the incorruptible, to be
absorbed in defined immensity, to offer oneself
to the fire and the transparency, to annihilate
oneself in proportion as one becomes more
deliberately conscious of oneself, and to give of
one's deepest to that whose depth has no end.

Teilhard de Chardin, SJ, 1881–1955

O Thou Supreme! most secret and most present, most beautiful and strong! What shall I

say, my God, my Life, my Holy Joy? What
shall any man say when he speaks of Thee?

St Augustine, 354–430

O God, your immensity fills the earth and the
whole universe, but the universe itself cannot
contain you, much less the earth, and still less
the world of my thoughts.   *Yves Raguin, SJ*

O Father, give the spirit power to climb
To the fountain of all light, and be purified.
Break through the mists of earth, the weight of
    the clod,
Shine forth in splendour, Thou that art calm
    weather,
And quiet resting place for faithful souls.
To see Thee is the end and the beginning,
Thou carriest us, and Thou dost go before,
Thou art the journey, and the journey's end.

Boethius, c.480–524

O God, let me rise to the edges of time and
    open my life to your eternity;
let me run to the edges of space and
    gaze into your immensity;
let me climb through the barriers of sound
    and pass into your silence;

9

And then, in stillness and silence
  let me adore You,
      Who are Life—Light—Love—
    without beginning and without end,
  the Source—the Sustainer—the Restorer—
    the Purifier—of all that is;
  the Lover who has bound earth to heaven
    by the beams of a cross;
  the Healer who has renewed a dying race
    by the blood of a chalice;
  the God who has taken man into your glory
    by the wounds of sacrifice;
God . . . God . . . God . . . Blessed be God
    Let me adore you.   *Sister Ruth, SLG*

God is what thought cannot better; God is
whom thought cannot reach; God no thinking
can even conceive. Without God, man can have
no being, no reason, no knowledge, no good
desire, naught. Thou, O God, art what thou art,
transcending all.   *Eric Milner-White, 1884–1964*

  Praise to the Holiest in the height,
    And in the depth be praise;
  In all his words most wonderful,
    Most sure in all his ways.

And that a higher gift than grace
 Should flesh and blood refine,
God's presence and his very self,
 And essence all-divine.

John Henry Newman, 1801–90

Blessed, praised and glorified,
 Exalted, extolled and honoured,
  Magnified and lauded
Be the name of the Holy One, blessed be he;

Though he be high above all the blessings and
   hymns,
 Praises and consolations,
 Which are uttered in the world;
 And say ye, Amen.

Authorized Daily Prayer Book (*Jewish*)

O come, let us sing unto the Lord: let us heartily
 rejoice in the strength of our salvation.
Let us come before his presence with thanksgiving: and shew ourselves glad in him with
 psalms.
For the Lord is a great God: and a great King
 above all gods.
In his hand are all the corners of the earth: and
 the strength of the hills is his also.

The sea is his, and he made it: and his hands
   prepared the dry land.

O come, let us worship and fall down: and kneel
   before the Lord our Maker.   *Psalm 95: 1–6*

Praise the Lord, O my soul: and all that is within
   me praise his holy Name.

Praise the Lord, O my soul: and forget not all
   his benefits;

Who forgiveth all thy sin: and healeth all thine
   infirmities;

Who saveth thy life from destruction: and
   crowneth thee with mercy and loving-
   kindness.   *Psalm 103: 1–4*

O God, my heart is ready; my heart is ready: I
   will sing and give praise with the best member
   that I have.

Awake, thou lute, and harp: I myself will awake
   right early.

I will give thanks unto thee, O Lord, among the
   people: I will sing praises unto thee among the
   nations.

For thy mercy is greater than the heavens: and
   thy truth reacheth unto the clouds.

                                      Psalm 108: 1–4

I thank thee, Father, Lord of heaven and earth, that thou hast hidden these things from the wise and understanding and revealed them to babes; yea, Father, for such was thy gracious will. All things have been delivered to me by my Father; and no one knows who the Son is except the Father, or who the Father is except the Son and anyone to whom the Son chooses to reveal him.

Luke 10: 21b–22

IN THE UPPER ROOM

Father, the hour has come; glorify thy Son that the Son may glorify thee . . .

I have manifested thy name to the men whom thou gavest me out of the world . . . I am praying for them . . . Holy Father, keep them in thy name, which thou hast given me, that they may be one, even as we are one . . . I do not pray that thou shouldst take them out of the world, but that thou shouldst keep them from the evil one . . . Sanctify them in the truth, thy word is truth . . . for their sake I consecrate myself, that they also may be consecrated in truth.

I do not pray for these only, but also for those who believe in me through their word, that they

may all be one, even as thou, Father, art in me,
and I in thee . . . that they also may be in us, so
that the world may believe that thou hast sent
me . . . and hast loved them even as thou hast
loved me. Father, I desire that they . . . may be
with me where I am, to behold my glory, which
thou hast given me . . . I have made known thy
name, and I will make it known, that the love
with which thou hast loved me may be in them,
and I in them.

From John 17

O the depths of the riches and wisdom and
knowledge of God! How unsearchable are his
judgments and how inscrutable his ways! For
who has known the mind of the Lord, or who
has been his counsellor? Or who has given a gift
to him that he might be repaid? For from him
and through him and to him are all things. To
him be glory for ever. Amen. *Romans 11: 33–6*

The Blessed and only Sovereign, the King of
kings and Lord of lords, who alone has immortality and dwells in unapproachable light,
whom no man has ever seen or can see. To him
be honour and eternal dominion. Amen.

1 Timothy 6: 15b–16

PETER'S THANKSGIVING FOR THE RESURRECTION

Blessed be the God and Father of our Lord Jesus Christ! By his great mercy we have been born anew to a living hope through the resurrection of Jesus Christ from the dead, and to an inheritance which is imperishable, undefiled, and unfading, kept in heaven for you, who by God's power are guarded through faith for a salvation ready to be revealed in the last time.

I Peter 1: 3–5

For this reason I bow my knees before the Father, from whom every family in heaven and on earth is named, that according to the riches of his glory he may grant you to be strengthened with might through his Spirit in the inner man, and that Christ may dwell in your hearts through faith; that you, being rooted and grounded in love, may have power to comprehend with all the saints what is the breadth and length and height and depth, and to know the love of Christ which surpasses knowledge, that you may be filled with all the fullness of God. Now to him who by the power at work within us is able to do far more abundantly than all that we

ask or think to him be glory in the church and in
Christ Jesus to all generations, for ever and ever.
Amen.   *Ephesians 3: 14–20*

O God, the God of all goodness and of all grace,
   who art worthy of a greater love
   than we can either give or understand:
Fill our hearts, we beseech thee,
    with such love toward thee
   that nothing may seem too hard for us to do
    or to suffer
   in obedience to thy will;
and grant that thus loving thee,
   we may become daily more like unto thee,
and finally obtain the crown of life
which thou hast promised to those that love
    thee;
   through Jesus Christ our Lord.
     Bishop Brooke Foss Westcott, 1825–1901

O Thou who through the light of nature hast
aroused in us a longing for the light of grace, so
that we may be raised in the light of Thy
majesty, to Thee, I give thanks, Creator and
Lord, that Thou allowest me to rejoice in Thy
works. Praise the Lord ye heavenly harmonies,
and ye who know the revealed harmonies. For

from Him, through Him and in Him, all is,
which is perceptible as well as spiritual; that
which we know and that which we do not know,
for there is still much to learn.

Johann Kepler, 1571–1630

God, of your goodness give me yourself for you
are sufficient for me. I cannot properly ask
anything less, to be worthy of you. If I were to
ask less, I should always be in want. In you alone
do I have all. *Julian of Norwich, 1342–1443*

Lord, thou that wilt not be seen but by those
that be clean of heart: I have done that in me is,
read and deeply thought and ensearched what it
is, and on what manner I might best come to this
cleanness that I might thee know somedeal.
Lord, I have sought and thought with all my
poor heart! And, Lord, in my meditation the
fire of desire kindled for to know thee, not only
the bitter bark without, but in feeling and
tasting in my soul. And this unworthiness I ask
not for me, for I am wretched and sinful and
most unworthy of all other. But, Lord, as a
whelp eateth of the crumbs that fall from the
board of his lord: of the heritage that is for to

come, a crop of that heavenly joy to comfort my
thirsty soul that burneth in love-longing to thee!

The Cloud of Unknowing, 14th century

Eternal Light, shine into our hearts,
Eternal Goodness, deliver us from evil,
Eternal Power, be our support,
Eternal Wisdom, scatter the darkness of our
ignorance,
Eternal Pity, have mercy upon us;
that with all our heart and mind and soul and
strength
we may seek thy face and be brought by thine
infinite mercy
to thy holy presence; through Jesus Christ our
Lord.   *Alcuin of York, 735–804*

Show us, good Lord,
the peace we should seek,
the peace we must give,
the peace we can keep,
the peace we must forgo,
and the peace you have given in Jesus our
Lord.

From Contemporary Prayers for Public Worship,
ed. Caryl Micklem

Prayer, the Church's banquet, Angels' age,
  God's breath in man returning to his birth,
The soul in paraphrase, heart in pilgrimage,
  The Christian plummet, sounding heaven
    and earth;
Engine against the Almighty, sinner's tower,
  Reversed thunder, Christ-side-piercing
    spear,
The six-days' world transposing in an hour,
  A kind of tune, which all things hear and fear;
Softness, and peace, and joy, and love, and
    bliss,
  Exalted manna, gladness of the best,
  Heaven in ordinary, man well drest,
The milky way, the bird of Paradise,
  Church-bells beyond the stars heard, the
    soul's blood,
  The land of spices; something understood.

George Herbert, 1593–1633

3

FORGIVENESS AND
PENITENCE

3. FORGIVENESS AND PENITENCE

God be merciful to me a sinner.   *Luke 18: 13*

I have gone astray like a sheep that is lost: O seek thy servant for I do not forget thy commandments.   *Ps. 119: 176*

Create and make in me a clean heart, O God, and renew a right spirit within me.   *Ps. 51: 10*

All have sinned and fall short of the glory of God.   *Romans 3: 23*

God in Heaven, you have helped my life to grow like a tree. Now something has happened. Satan, like a bird, has carried in one twig of his own choosing after another. Before I knew it he had built a dwelling-place and was living in it. Tonight, my Father, I am throwing out both the bird and the nest.   *Prayer of a Nigerian Christian*

O thou great Chief, light a candle in my heart, that I may see what is therein, and sweep the rubbish from thy dwelling-place.

   An African schoolgirl's prayer

Almighty God, Spirit of purity and grace, in asking thy forgiveness I cannot claim a right to

be forgiven but only cast myself upon thine
unbounded love.

 I can plead no merit or desert:
 I can plead no extenuating circumstances:
 I cannot plead the frailty of my nature:
 I cannot plead the force of the temptations I
  encounter:
 I cannot plead the persuasions of others who
  led me astray:
 I can only say, for the sake of Jesus Christ thy
  Son, my Lord.   Amen.

John Baillie, 1886–1960

As the first martyr prayed to thee for his
murderers, O Lord, so we fall before thee and
pray; forgive all who hate and maltreat us and let
not one of them perish because of us, but may all
be saved by thy grace, O God the all-bountiful.

Eastern Church

O Lord, remember not only the men and
women of good will, but also those of ill will.
But do not remember all the suffering they
have inflicted on us; remember the fruits we
have bought, thanks to this suffering—our
comradeship, our loyalty, our humility, our
courage, our generosity, the greatness of heart

which has grown out of all this, and when they come to judgement let all the fruits which we have borne be their forgiveness.

Prayer written by an unknown prisoner in Ravensbrück concentration camp and left by the body of a dead child

Blessed Lord, who wast tempted in all things like as we are, have mercy upon our frailty. Out of weakness give us strength. Grant to us thy fear, that we may fear thee only. Support us in time of temptation. Embolden us in the time of danger. Help us to do thy work with good courage; and to continue thy faithful soldiers and servants unto our life's end; through Jesus Christ our Lord.

Bishop Brooke Foss Westcott, 1825–1901

Our God and God of our fathers, let our prayer reach You—do not turn away from our pleading. For we are not so arrogant and obstinate to claim that we are indeed righteous people and have never sinned. But we know that both we and our fathers have sinned.

We have abused and betrayed. We are cruel.

We have destroyed and embittered other people's lives.

We were false to ourselves.

24

We have gossiped about others and hated
them.

We have insulted and jeered. We have killed.
We have lied.

We have misled others and neglected them.

We were obstinate. We have perverted and
quarrelled.

We have robbed and stolen.

We have transgressed through unkindness.

We have been both violent and weak.

We have practised extortion.

We have yielded to wrong desires, our zeal
was misplaced.

We turn away from Your commandments and
good judgement but it does not help us. Your
justice exists whatever happens to us, for You
work for truth, but we bring about evil. What
can we say before You—so distant is the place
where You are found? And what can we tell
You—Your being is remote as the heavens? Yet
You know everything, hidden and revealed.
You know the mysteries of the universe and the
intimate secrets of everyone alive. You probe
our body's state. You see into the heart and
mind. Nothing escapes You, nothing is hidden
from Your gaze. Our God and God of our
fathers, have mercy on us and pardon all our

sins; grant atonement for all our iniquities,
forgiveness for all our transgressions.

Jewish Day of Atonement

MAN'S NEED OF GRACE

As a fish that is dragged from the water
Gaspeth,
So gaspeth my soul:

As one who hath buried his treasure,
And now cannot find the place,
So is my mind distraught:

As a child that hath lost his mother,
So am I troubled, my heart is seared with sore
anguish:

O merciful God,
Thou knowest my need,
Come, save me, and show me Thy love.

Tukaram, 1608-1649

This is my prayer to thee, my lord—strike,
strike at the root of penury in my heart.
Give me the strength lightly to bear my joys and
sorrows.
Give me the strength to make my love fruitful in
service.

Give me the strength never to disown the poor
    or bend my knees before insolent might.
Give me the strength to raise my mind high
    above daily trifles.
And give me the strength to surrender my
    strength to thy will with love.

Rabindranath Tagore, 1861–1941

May God who pardoned David through Nathan
the prophet when he confessed his sins, and
Peter weeping bitterly for his denial, and the
sinful woman weeping at his feet, and the
publican and the prodigal son, may the same
God forgive thee all things, through me a sinner,
both in this world and in the world to come, and
set thee uncondemned before his terrible judgement seat. Have no further care for the sins
which thou hast confessed, depart in peace.

Absolution, Orthodox

Grandfather,
Look at our brokenness.

We know that in all creation
Only the human family
Has strayed from the Sacred Way.

We know that we are the ones
Who are divided
And we are the ones
Who must come back together
To walk in the Sacred Way.

Grandfather,
Sacred One,
Teach us love, compassion, and honour
That we may heal the earth
And heal each other.   *Ojibway people of Canada*

All that we ought to have thought and have
    not thought,
All that we ought to have said, and have not
    said,
All that we ought to have done, and have not
    done;
All that we ought not to have thought, and
    yet have thought,
All that we ought not to have spoken, and yet
    have spoken,
All that we ought not to have done, and yet
    have done;
For thoughts, words and works, pray we, O
    God, for forgiveness.

From an ancient Persian prayer

4

THE LORD'S PRAYER

4. THE LORD'S PRAYER

OUR FATHER

Let me depend on God alone:
    who never changes,
    who knows what is best for me
      so much better than I;
and gives in a thousand ways, at all times
    all that the perfect Father can
      for the son's good growth,
    things needful, things salutary,
    things wise, beneficent and happy.

Eric Milner-White, 1884–1964

O Lord Jesus Christ, Thou Word and Revelation of the Eternal Father, come, we pray Thee, take possession of our hearts, and reign where Thou hast right to reign. So fill our minds with the thought and our imaginations with the picture of Thy love, that there may be in us no room for any desire that is discordant with Thy holy will. Cleanse us, we pray Thee, from all that may make us deaf to Thy call or slow to obey it, Who, with the Father and the Holy Spirit, art one God, blessed for ever.

William Temple, 1881–1944

The Lord's Prayer

IN HEAVEN

I believe that God is real,
Even though I cannot realize Him;
That what I commit to Him, He will glorify, and
    use for his eternal purpose.
I believe that his will is love to all of us.
His ways are not our ways,
But we may come to Him
    Through Jesus,
    Through his Spirit,
    Through all beauty, love and truth.

Margaret Cropper, 1886–1980

As the rain hides the stars, as the autumn mist
hides the hills, as the clouds veil the blue of the
sky, so the dark happenings of my lot hide the
shining of thy face from me. Yet, if I may hold
thy hand in the darkness, it is enough. Since I
know that, though I may stumble in my going,
thou dost not fall.   *Gaelic, tr. Alistair MacLean*

HALLOWED BE YOUR NAME

   . . . Blessed be thy holy Name,
     O Lord, my God!
For ever blessed be thy holy Name,
     For that I am made

31

The Lord's Prayer

The work of thy hands,
Curiously wrought
    By thy divine Wisdom,
Enriched
    By thy Goodness,
Being more thine
Than I am mine own.
    O Lord!

Thomas Traherne, 1636–74

Bishop Serapion's Prayer of Oblation

We praise you, Father, invisible, Giver of immortality. You are the source of life and light, the source of all grace and truth; you love men and you love the poor, you seek reconciliation with all men and draw them all to you by sending your dear Son to visit them.

May the Lord Jesus and the Holy Spirit speak in us and praise you through us, for you are high above all princedoms, powers, virtues and dominations, above everything that can be named, both in this world and in the world to come . . .

Holy, holy, holy is the Lord of hosts. Heaven and earth are full of your glory. Heaven is full, earth is full of your wonderful glory . . .

Bishop Serapion, 4th century

YOUR KINGDOM COME

Eternal God, in whose perfect kingdom no
sword is drawn but the sword of righteousness,
and no strength known but the strength of
love . . . We pray thee so mightily to shed and
spread abroad thy Spirit, that all peoples and
ranks may be gathered under one banner, of the
Prince of Peace; as children of one God and
Father of all; to whom be dominion and glory
now and for ever.   Amen.

Eric Milner-White, 1884–1964

Almighty God, from whom all thoughts of truth
and peace proceed, kindle, we pray thee, in the
hearts of all men the true love of peace, and
guide with thy pure and peaceable wisdom
those who take counsel for the nations of the
earth; that in tranquillity thy kingdom may go
forward, till the earth be filled with the knowledge of thy love; through Jesus Christ our
Lord.   *Francis Paget, Bishop of Oxford, 1851–1911*

YOUR WILL BE DONE

O Lord God
when we pray unto thee
    desiring well and meaning truly,

33

if thou seest a better way
    to thy glory and our good,
then be thy will done,
    and not ours:
as with thy dear Son
    in the Garden of Agony,
even Jesus Christ our Lord.

Eric Milner-White, 1884–1964

Lord, I thank you for teaching me how to live in
the present moment. In this way I enjoy each
simple task as I do it without thinking that I
must hurry on to the next thing. I do what I am
doing with all my ability and all my concentration. My mind is no longer divided, and life is
more peaceful. Thank you for teaching me how
to do this, and please help me how to show
others the way to learn to trust you more
completely and to do everything which has to be
done at your time and your speed.

Michael Hollings and Etta Gullick

GIVE US TODAY OUR DAILY BREAD

Lord God, we thank you for all the good things
of your providing, and we pray for the time
when people everywhere shall have the

abundant life of your will, revealed to us in Jesus
Christ, your Son, our Lord. *G.A.*

Blessed are you, Lord, God of all creation.
Through your goodness we have this bread to
offer, which earth has given and human hands
have made. It will become for us the bread of
life.

Blessed are you, Lord, God of all creation.
Through your goodness we have this wine to
offer, fruit of the vine and work of human
hands. It will become our spiritual drink.

Offertory prayers, The Roman Missal

FORGIVE US OUR SINS

Almighty God, Spirit of purity and grace, in
asking thy forgiveness I cannot claim a right to
be forgiven but only cast myself upon thine
unbounded love.

I can plead no merit or desert:
I can plead no extenuating circumstances:
I cannot plead the frailty of my nature:
I cannot plead the force of the temptations I
encounter:

I cannot plead the persuasions of others who
    led me astray:
I can only say, for the sake of Jesus Christ thy
    Son, my Lord.   Amen.

                  John Baillie, 1886–1960

Lord, today you made us known to friends we
    did not know,
And you have given us seats in homes which are
    not our own.
You have brought the distant near,
And made a brother of a stranger,
Forgive us Lord . . .
We did not introduce you.   *Prayer from Polynesia*

AS WE FORGIVE THOSE WHO SIN AGAINST
US

O Lord, remember not only the men and
women of good will, but also those of ill will.
But do not remember all the suffering they
have inflicted on us; remember the fruits we
have bought, thanks to this suffering—our
comradeship, our loyalty, our humility, our
courage, our generosity, the greatness of heart
which has grown out of all this, and when they

come to judgement let all the fruits which we
have borne be their forgiveness.

*Prayer written by an unknown prisoner in Ravensbrück
concentration camp and left by the body of a dead child*

O Lord give me strength to refrain from the
unkind silence that is born of hardness of heart;
the unkind silence that clouds the serenity of
understanding and is the enemy of peace.

Give me strength to be the first to tender the
healing word and the renewal of friendship, that
the bonds of amity and the flow of charity may
be strengthened for the good of the brethren and
the furthering of thine eternal, loving purpose.

Cecil Hunt

LEAD US NOT INTO TEMPTATION

From the cowardice that dare not face new truth
From the laziness that is contented with half
truth
From the arrogance that thinks it knows all
truth,
Good Lord, deliver me.   *Prayer from Kenya*

The Lord's Prayer

Lord God Almighty,
I pray thee for thy great mercy and by the token
    of the holy rood,
Guide me to thy will, to my soul's need, better
    than I can myself;
And shield me against my foes, seen and
    unseen;
And teach me to do thy will
    that I may inwardly love thee before all things
    with a clean mind and a clean body.
For thou art my maker and my redeemer,
    my help, my comfort, my trust, and my hope.
Praise and glory be to thee now, ever and ever,
    world without end.   *King Alfred, 849–901*

BUT DELIVER US FROM EVIL

Blessed are all thy Saints, O God and King, who
have travelled over the tempestuous sea of this
mortal life, and have made the harbour of peace
and felicity. Watch over us who are still in our
dangerous voyage; and remember such as lie
exposed to the rough storms of trouble and
temptations. Frail is our vessel, and the ocean is
wide; but as in thy mercy thou hast set our
course, so steer the vessel of our life toward the
everlasting shore of peace, and bring us at

length to the quiet haven of our heart's desire,
where thou, O our God, are blessed, and livest
and reignest for ever and ever.

St Augustine, 354–430

Guard for me my eyes, Jesus Son of Mary, lest
seeing another's wealth make me covetous.

Guard for me my ears, lest they hearken to
slander, lest they listen constantly to folly in
the sinful world.

Guard for me my heart, O Christ, in thy love,
lest I ponder wretchedly the desire of any
iniquity.

Guard for me my hands, that they be not
stretched out for quarrelling, that they may
not, after that, practise shameful supplica-
tion.

Guard for me my feet upon the gentle earth of
Ireland, lest, bent on profitless errands, they
abandon rest.   *Irish*

FOR THINE IS THE KINGDOM

O Christ, who laid aside your glory and lived as a
man, that all men might see the light of God
shining through a human life; help us to be more
like you and to lay aside all that hides you from

the peoples of other races—our pride of race, of knowledge, of civilization; so that through our lives of prayer and communion and love, they may come to see you as you are, and hail you as their Lord.

Sister Ruth, SLG

O God, the God of all goodness and of all grace, who art worthy of a greater love than we can either give or understand, fill our hearts, we beseech thee, with such love toward thee, that nothing may seem too hard for us to do or to suffer in obedience to thy will; and grant that thus loving thee, we may become daily more like unto thee, and finally obtain the crown of life which thou hast promised to those that love thee; through Jesus Christ our Lord.

Farnham Hostel Manual, 19th century

THE POWER AND THE GLORY

O come, Holy Spirit, inflame my heart, set it on fire with love. Burn away my self-centredness so that I can love unselfishly. Breathe your life-giving breath into my soul so that I can live freely and joyously, unrestricted by self-consciousness, and may be ready to go wherever you may send me. Come like a gentle breeze and give me your still peace so that I may be quiet and know the wonder of your presence, and help diffuse it in the world. Never let me shut you out; never let me try to limit you to my capacity; act freely in me and through me, never leave me, O Lord and giver of life!

Michael Hollings and Etta Gullick

O Holy Spirit,
    Giver of light and life,
impart to us thoughts higher than our own
        thoughts,
    and prayers better than our own prayers,
    and powers beyond our own powers,
that we may spend and be spent
in the ways of love and goodness,
    after the perfect image
of our Lord and Saviour Jesus Christ.

Eric Milner-White, 1884–1964, and G. W. Briggs, 1875–1959

FOR EVER AND EVER

Give me thy grace, good Lord, to make death no stranger to me. Give me, good Lord, a longing to be with thee, not for the avoiding of the calamities of this wretched world; nor so much

41

for the avoiding of the pains of purgatory, nor of the pains of hell neither, nor so much for the attaining of the joys of heaven in respect of mine own commodity, as even for a very love to thee.

St Thomas More, 1475–1535

We thank thee, O God, for the saints of all ages; for those who in times of darkness kept the lamp of faith burning; for the great souls who saw visions of larger truth and dared to declare it; for the multitude of quiet and gracious souls whose presence has purified and sanctified the world; and for those known and loved by us, who have passed from this earthly fellowship into the fuller light of life with thee. *Anon.*

5

THE EUCHARIST

5. THE EUCHARIST

'What could be more ridiculous than the
Eucharist?'
A. J. Ayer

'I could be wrong. I'm not omniscient.'
A. J. Ayer

Let all mortal flesh keep silence, and with fear
    and trembling stand;
Ponder nothing earthly-minded, for with bles-
    sings in his hand,
Christ our God to earth descendeth, our full
    homage to command.   *Liturgy of St James*

Lord, this is thy feast,
    prepared by thy longing,
    spread at thy command,
    attended at thine invitation,
    blessed by thine own Word,
    distributed by thine own hand,
    the undying memorial of thy sacrifice
        upon the Cross,
    the full gift of thine everlasting love,
    and its perpetuation till time shall end.
Lord, this is Bread of heaven,
    Bread of life,

that, whoso eateth, never shall hunger more
And this the cup of pardon, healing, glad-
     ness, strength,
  that whoso drinketh, thirsteth not again.

So may we come, O Lord, to thy table;
  Lord Jesus, come to us.

Eric Milner-White, 1884–1964

Blessed are you, Lord, God of all creation.
Through your goodness we have this bread to
offer, which earth has given and human hands
have made. It will become for us the bread of
life.
Blessed are you, Lord, God of all creation.
Through your goodness we have this wine to
offer, fruit of the vine and work of human
hands. It will become our spiritual drink.

Offertory prayers, The Roman Missal

We offer you, O Lord our God, the gifts
commanded by your blessed Son, and pray that
they may be both symbol and reality of the
divine life which You share with us your other
children, feeding and nourishing our souls unto
eternal life. Blessed be You for ever.

G.A.

The Eucharist

Godhead here in hiding, whom I do adore
Masked by these bare shadows, shape and
    nothing more,
See, Lord, at thy service low lies here a heart
Lost, all lost in wonder at the God thou art . . .

Jesu whom I look at shrouded here below,
I beseech thee send me what I thirst for so,
Some day to gaze on thee face to face in light
And be blest for ever with thy glory's sight.

Latin, 13th century, tr. Gerard Manley Hopkins, 1844–89

The word went forth
Yet from his Father never went away:
Came to his work on earth
And laboured till the twilight of his day.

Men envied him: he went to death
By his own man betrayed:
Yet first to his own men himself had given,
In wine and broken bread.

O victim slain for us and our salvation,
Opening the door of light,
The warring hosts are set on our damnation:
Give us the strength to fight.

St Thomas Aquinas, 1225–74

The Eucharist

Holy things for those who would be holy.
Heavenly food for the spiritually hungry. Let us
draw near in faith and love with thanksgiving.

For the bread that we have eaten
For the wine that we have tasted
For the life that you have given:
    Father, Son and Holy Spirit,
    We will praise you.

For the life of Christ within us
Turning all our fears to freedom
Helping us to live for others:
    Father, Son and Holy Spirit,
    We will praise you.

For the strength of Christ to lead us
In our living and our dying,
In the end with all your people
    Father, Son and Holy Spirit,
    We will praise you.

Brian Wren: from Contemporary Prayers for Public
Worship, *ed. Caryl Micklem*

Strengthen, O Lord, the hands that holy things
have taken, that they may daily bring forth fruit
to thy glory. Grant, O Lord, that the lips which
have sung thy praise within the sanctuary, may
glorify thee for ever; that the ears which have

heard the voice of thy songs, may be closed to
the voice of clamour and dispute; that the eyes
which have seen thy great love, may also behold
thy blessed hope; that the tongues which have
sung the sanctus, may ever speak the truth.
Grant that the feet that have trod in thy holy
courts may ever walk in the light, and that the
souls and bodies, which have tasted of thy living
body and blood, may ever be restored in
newness of life.   *Liturgy of Malabar*

O God, who hast brought us near to an
innumerable company of angels and to the
spirits of just men made perfect; grant us in our
pilgrimage to abide in their fellowship, and in
our heavenly country to become partakers of
their joy; through Jesus Christ our Lord.

William Bright, 1824–1901

Finished and perfected, so far as we are able, is
    the mystery of thy incarnate work, O Christ
    our God.
For we have kept the memorial of thy death,
We have seen the figure of thy resurrection,
We have been filled with thine unending life,
We have rejoiced in thine unfailing joy.

Grant that we may be counted worthy of that
  same joy also in the age to come.

Liturgy of St Basil the Great

Love bade me welcome; yet my soul drew back,
  Guilty of dust and sin.
But quick-eyed Love, observing me grow slack
  From my first entrance in,
Drew nearer to me, sweetly questioning
  If I lack'd anything.

'A guest,' I answer'd, 'worthy to be here:'
  Love said, 'You shall be he.'
'I, the unkind, ungrateful? Ah, my dear,
  I cannot look on Thee.'
Love took my hand and smiling did reply,
  'Who made the eyes but I?'

'Truth, Lord, but I have marr'd them: let my
    shame
  Go where it doth deserve.'
'And know you not,' says Love, 'Who bore the
    blame?'
  'My dear, then I will serve.'
'You must sit down,' says Love, 'and taste my
    meat.'
  So I did sit and eat.   *George Herbert, 1593–1633*

6

LISTENING TO GOD

6. LISTENING TO GOD

Prayer is relationship with God. Such relationship presupposes communication from both sides. Not only does a person pray to God in words or unspoken thoughts, but also God communicates with the praying one in intuitions, often so clear that they can be interpreted into direct speech. At such times God's initiative is clearly apparent, and the heart is moved to respond in prayer or silent worship, or in inspired and obedient word or action.

Abraham, the founding patriarch of biblical religion: 'The Lord said to Abram, "Go from your country and your kindred and your father's house to the land that I will show you. And I will make of you a great nation . . . and by you all the families of the earth shall bless themselves." '   *Genesis 12: 1-3*

Moses at the burning bush: 'God called to him out of the bush . . . "I am the God of your father, the God of Abraham, the God of Isaac and the God of Jacob . . . I have seen the affliction of my people who are in Egypt . . . I

will send you to Pharaoh . . . I AM WHO I AM."
Say "I AM has sent me to you." ' *Exodus 3: 4–14*

Elijah at the cave on Horeb: 'after the wind . . .
the earthquake . . . and the fire, a still small
voice, "What are you doing here, Elijah? . . .
Go, return on your way to the wilderness of
Damascus . . .".' *1 Kings 19: 11–15*

Job, seeking to understand the mystery of
suffering, argued with God and with his 'com-
forters': 'Then the Lord answered Job out of the
whirlwind: "Where were you when I laid the
foundations of the earth? Tell me, if you have
understanding . . . Shall a faultfinder contend
with the Almighty? . . . Will you even put me in
the wrong . . . that you may be justified? . . ."
Then Job answered the Lord, "I have uttered
what I did not understand . . . I had heard of
thee by the hearing of the ear, but now my eye
sees thee; therefore I despise myself and re-
pent . . .".' *Job 38: 1, 4; 40: 2, 8; 42: 3–6*

Isaiah, after his vision in the Temple: 'I heard
the voice of the Lord saying, "Whom shall I
send, and who will go for us?" Then I said,
"Here am I! send me." '

'Thus says the high and lofty One . . . "I dwell in the high and holy place, and also with him who is of a contrite and humble spirit".'

Isaiah 6: 8; 57: 15

Hosea: 'What shall I do with you, O Ephraim? What shall I do with you, O Judah? Your love is like a morning cloud, like the dew that goes early away . . . I desire steadfast love and not sacrifice, the knowledge of God rather than burnt offerings.'

Hosea 6: 4, 6

Micah speaks for the Lord: 'He has showed you, O man, what is good: and what does the Lord require of you but to do justice and to love kindness, and to walk humbly with your God?'

Micah 6: 8

Jeremiah: 'The word of the Lord came to me saying, "Before I formed you in the womb I knew you, and before you were born I consecrated you; I appointed you a prophet to the nations." . . . "Ah, Lord God, behold I do not know how to speak, for I am only a youth." . . . "Do not say, 'I am only a youth'; for to all to whom I send you, you shall go, and whatever I command you you shall speak.'"

Jeremiah 1: 4–7

Jonah resented Nineveh's repentance and the withering of the gourd: 'And the Lord said, "Do you do well to be angry?" . . . "I do well to be angry, angry enough to die." And the Lord said, "You pity the plant, for which you did not labour . . . [and] which came into being in a night, and perished in a night. And should not I pity Nineveh, that great city, in which there are more than a hundred and twenty thousand persons who do not know their right hand from their left, and also much cattle?"'

Jonah 4: 4, 9b–11

Mary of Nazareth heard the Angel's annunciation: 'You will conceive . . . and bear a son, and you shall call his name Jesus.' . . . And Mary said ". . . I am the handmaid of the Lord; let it be to me according to your word."'

Luke 1: 31, 38

Jesus, after his baptism: 'a voice came from heaven, "Thou art my beloved Son; with thee I am well pleased."'

at his transfiguration: 'a voice came out of the cloud, "This is my beloved Son; listen to him."'

after his entry into Jerusalem: '"Now is my soul troubled. And what shall I say? 'Father, save me from this hour'? No, for this purpose I have come to this hour. Father, glorify thy name." Then a voice came from heaven, "I have glorified it, and I will glorify it again."'

Mark 1: 11; Mark 9: 7; John 12: 27, 28

Saul of Tarsus, struck blind on the road to Damascus, 'heard a voice saying to him, "Saul, Saul, why do you persecute me?" And he said, "Who are you, Lord?" And he said, "I am Jesus, whom you are persecuting".'

Acts 9: 4–5

John on Patmos, heard the words: '"I am the first and the last, and the living one; I died, and behold I am alive for evermore, and I have the keys of Death and Hades."'

Later a great voice from the throne said: '"Behold, the dwelling of God is with men . . . and they shall be his people . . . he will wipe away every tear from their eyes, and death shall be no more, neither shall there be mourning nor crying nor pain any more, for the former things

have passed away . . . Behold, I make all things new.'"
Revelation 1: 17–18; 21: 3, 4, 5

Antony of Egypt (3rd century): God spoke to him through the Gospel read in Church: 'If thou wilt be perfect, go, sell all that thou hast and give to the poor, and take up thy cross and follow me.'

Later, experiencing the direct conflict with evil, he cried out, 'Where were you, Lord, while I went through such tribulations?' A voice answered, 'I was here by your side, Antony, I have never left you . . . I will be your guide and comforter . . .'

Francis of Assisi (early 13th century), while praying before the crucifix in the ruined church of San Damiano, heard the words: 'Francis, go, repair my house, which, as you see, is falling completely to ruin.'

Thomas Aquinas (13th century), when pressed by his secretary, Reginald of Piperno, to explain why he had broken off his unfinished work, the *Summa Theologica*, said: 'All that I have written seems like straw compared to what has now been revealed to me.'

According to tradition in his vision he heard the Lord say, 'Thomas, you have written well of me: what shall be your reward?' and his reply was, 'No reward but yourself, Lord.'

Julian of Norwich (14th century): When she was 30 years old this anchoress had a serious illness which she had prayed God to send her, during which she received sixteen 'revelations of divine love', on which she meditated for the rest of her life.

'Then said our good Lord Jesus Christ:

' "I am ground of thy beseeching . . . Pray inwardly, though thee thinketh it savour thee not: for it is profitable, though thou feel not . . ."

' "Thou shalt not be overcome", was said full clearly . . . He said not, "Thou shalt not be tempested, thou shalt not be travailed, thou shalt not be dis-eased", but he said, "Thou shalt not be overcome".'

Revelations of Divine Love

Dag Hammarskjöld (20th century): 'I don't know who—or what—put the question, I don't know when it was put. I don't even remember answering. But at some moment I did answer

Yes to Someone—or Something—and from that hour I was certain that existence is meaningful and that, therefore, my life in self-surrender, had a goal. From that moment I have known what it means "not to look back", and "to take no thought for the morrow".'

Markings

Simone Weil (20th century): 'I heard by chance of the existence of those English poets of the seventeenth century who are named metaphysical. I discovered the poem . . . called "Love". I learnt it by heart. Often . . . I make myself say it over, concentrating all my attention upon it, and clinging with all my soul to the tenderness it enshrines. I used to think I was merely reciting it as a beautiful poem, but without my knowing it the recitation had the virtue of a prayer. It was during one of these recitations that, as I told you, Christ himself came down and took possession of me.

'Until last September I had never once prayed to God in all my life.'

Waiting on God

King David speaks of the effect of listening to God:

'The Spirit of the Lord speaks by me,
his word is upon my tongue.
The God of Israel has spoken,
the Rock of Israel has said to me:
When one rules justly over men,
ruling in the fear of God,
he dawns on them like the morning light,
like the sun shining forth upon a cloudless
    morning,
like rain that makes grass to sprout from the
    earth.'
                            2 Samuel 23: 2–4

7

PRAYING FOR THE WORLD

7. PRAYING FOR THE WORLD

For God so loved the world that He gave his only Son that whosoever believes in him should not perish but have eternal life. For God sent the Son into the world, not to condemn the world, but that the world might be saved through him.

John 3: 16

And God saw everything that He had made, and behold, it was very good. *Genesis 1: 31*

Lead us, O God, from the sight of the lovely things of the world to the thought of thee their Creator; and grant that delighting in the beautiful things of thy creation we may delight in thee, the first author of beauty and the Sovereign Lord of all thy works, blessed for evermore.

G.A.

O Almighty God, the Father of all mankind, we pray thee to turn to thyself the hearts of all peoples and their rulers, that by the power of thy Holy Spirit peace may be established on the foundation of justice, righteousness and truth; through Him who was lifted up on the cross to

draw all men unto Himself, even thy Son Jesus
Christ our Lord.   *William Temple, 1881–1944*

Pour thy blessing, O God, we pray thee, upon
Elizabeth our Queen that she may fulfil her
calling as a Christian ruler. Support her in the
ceaseless round of duty, inspire her in the
service of many peoples. Give her wise and
selfless ministers, bless her in home and family,
and grant that through her the Commonwealth
may be knit together in one great brotherhood, a
strength and joy to all its members and an
instrument of peace in our troubled world,
through Jesus Christ, our Lord.   *G.A.*

Grant, O Lord, that thy Spirit may permeate
every sphere of human thought and activity.
Let those who believe in thee take with them
into their daily work the values of thy kingdom,
the insights of the gospel and the love of their
fellow-men. Hasten the time when justice and
brotherhood shall be established and when all
men shall be brought into the unity of thy Son,
our Saviour Jesus Christ.   *G.A.*

O Lord, I remember before thee tonight all the
  workers of the world:

Workers with hand or brain:
Workers in cities or in the fields:
Men who go forth to toil and women who keep
    house:
Employers and employees:
Those who command and those who obey:
Those whose work is dangerous:
Those whose work is monotonous or mean:
Those who can find no work to do:
Those whose work is the service of the poor
Or the healing of the sick
Or the proclamation of the gospel of Christ
At home or in foreign places.

John Baillie, 1886–1960

Let the healing grace of your love, O Lord, so
transform me that I may play my part in the
transfiguration of the world from a place of
suffering, death and corruption to a realm of
infinite light, joy and love. Make me so obedient
to your Spirit that my life may become a living
prayer, and a witness to your unfailing presence.

Martin Israel

O Lord Jesus our God
Who called people from their daily work
Saying to them 'Come ye after me',

Praying for the World

May your children today hear your voice
   And gladly answer your call
   To give their lives to you
   To serve your Church
   To offer their gifts
   And give away their hearts
   To you only.

   Bless their hopes
The first tiny stirrings of desire
The little resolve to go forward
The small vision of what might be.

   Deal gently with their fears
The hesitation of uncertainty
The darkness of the unknown
The lack of confidence in their own capacity
   And turn it all to trust in you.

*Gabrielle Hadingham, United Society
for the Propagation of the Gospel*

AT THE DOOR OF A CHRISTIAN HOSPITAL

O God,
make the door of this house wide enough
to receive all who need human love and
fellowship, and a heavenly Father's care;
   and narrow enough to shut out
all envy, pride and hate.

65

Praying for the World

Make its threshold smooth enough
to be no stumbling-block to children,
nor to straying feet,
    but rugged enough to turn back
the tempter's power:
    make it a gateway
    to thine eternal kingdom.

Bishop Thomas Ken, 1637–1711

O God of goodness,
in the mystery of natural disasters we look to
    thee,
trusting that there is an explanation that will
satisfy our minds and hearts.
Accept our compassion for our fellow-men,
our desire for their relief,
and our hope for knowledge which shall control
the forces of nature.
Help us to help thee complete thy universe,
O creator Father,
to remove its flaws,
so that we may be sub-creators with thee of the
Kingdom of thy love in Jesus Christ.   *G.A.*

O Supreme Eternal Reality, Pure Being beyond
all subject and object, beyond all cerebral thinking, Unconceptualizable and Unverbalizable,

dwelling in silence, I long to experience the
nameless, incomprehensible being, as Moses
did at the Burning Bush, burning and never
consumed, a higher consciousness, before
which I can only bow in silence and reverence,
glimpsing indescribable suchness and eternal
mystery.   *Anon. A Christian tries to pray in Zen terms*

O God,
Let us be united;
Let us speak in harmony;
Let our minds apprehend alike.
Common be our prayer;
Common be the end of our assembly;
Common be our resolution;
Common be our deliberations.
Alike be our feelings;
Unified be our hearts;
Common be our intentions;
Perfect be our unity. *Hindu Scriptures* (Rig-Veda)

O bless this people, Lord, who seek their own
   face
under the mask and can hardly recognize it . . .
O bless this people that breaks its bond . . .

And with them, all the peoples of Europe,
All the peoples of Asia,
All the peoples of Africa,
All the peoples of America,
Who sweat blood and sufferings.

And see, in the midst of these millions of waves
The sea swell of the heads of my people.
And grant to their warm hands that they may
    clasp
The earth in a girdle of brotherly hands,
Beneath the rainbow of thy peace.

Leopold Sedar Senghor

We offer our thanks to thee
    for sending thy only Son to die for us all
In a world divided by colour bars,
    how sweet a thing it is to know
    that in thee we all belong to one family.
There are times when we
        unprivileged people,
    weep tears that are not loud but deep,
    when we think of the suffering we experi-
        ence.
We come to thee, our only hope and refuge.
Help us, O God, to refuse to be embittered
    against those who handle us with harshness.

Praying for the World

We are grateful to thee
for the gift of laughter at all times.
Save us from hatred of those who oppress us.
May we follow the spirit of thy Son Jesus Christ.

A Bantu pastor

Gather us in, Thou love that fillest all;
Gather our rival faiths within thy fold.
Rend each man's temple-veil and bid it fall,
That we may know that Thou hast been of old;
         Gather us in.

Gather us in: we worship only Thee;
In varied names we stretch a common hand;
In diverse forms a common soul we see;
In many ships we seek one spirit-land;
         Gather us in.

Each sees one colour of thy rainbow-light,
Each looks upon one tint and calls it heaven;
Thou art the fullness of our partial sight;
We are not perfect till we find the seven;
         Gather us in.

G. D. Matheson, 1842–1906

By the grace of God's Name
May humanity find itself lifted higher and
higher.

Praying for the World

In thy dispensation O Lord,
Let there be good in all humanity.

Guru Nanak, 1489–1559, founder of Sikhism

O thou whose divine tenderness ever outsoars
the narrow loves and charities of earth, grant me
today a kind and gentle heart towards all things
that live. Let me not ruthlessly hurt any
creature of thine. Let me take thought also for
the welfare of little children, and of those who
are sick, and of the poor; remembering that
what I do unto the least of these his brethren I do
unto Jesus Christ my Lord.

John Baillie, 1886–1960

Our God and God of our fathers,
Reign over the whole universe in thy glory,
And in Thy splendour be exalted over all the
earth.
Shine forth in the majesty of thy triumphant
strength,
Over all the inhabitants of thy world,
That every form may know that Thou hast
formed it,
And every creature understand that Thou hast
created it,

And that all that hath breath in its nostrils may
    say:
    The Lord God of Israel is King
    And his dominion ruleth over all.

New Year Liturgy

Eternal God, whose image lies in the hearts of all
    people,
We live among peoples whose ways are different
    from ours,
    whose faiths are foreign to us,
    whose tongues are unintelligible to us.
Help us to remember that you love all people
    with your great love,
    that all religion is an attempt to respond to
    you,
    that the yearnings of other hearts are much
    like our own and are known to you.
Help us to recognize you in the words of truth,
    the things of beauty, the actions of love
    about us.
We pray through Christ, who is a stranger to no
    one land more than another, and to every
    land no less than to another.

World Council of Churches, Vancouver Assembly, 1983

Praying for the World

I shall sing a song of praise to God:
Strike the chords upon the drum.
God who gives us all good things—
Strike the chords upon the drum—
Wives, and wealth, and wisdom.
Strike the chords upon the drum.

Baluba, Zaïre

Prayer For The City

God of the city, God of the tenement and the
houses of the rich, God of the subway and the
night-club, God of the cathedral and the streets,
God of the sober and the drunk, the junkie and
the stripper, the gambler and the good family
man; dear God, help us to see the world and its
children through your eyes, and to love accord-
ingly.

Monica Furlong, Dawn through our Darkness

Completing The Universe

Astronomers tell us that galaxies of stars are still
being brought into existence millions of light
years away in infinite space. Evidently creation
is still going on. Natural catastrophes still take
place, the causes of which have still to be
discovered. For the present, incurable diseases
take toll of many lives. Clearly there are flaws in

the universe that need to be set right or avoided. Men now have the ability to alter the course of rivers, to build dams, to irrigate deserts, desalinate sea water. Modern man can co-operate with God in completing the universe, in a way of which previous generations had no idea.

G.A. Journey for a Soul

8

PRAYING FOR THE CHURCH

8. PRAYING FOR THE CHURCH

But you are a chosen race, a royal priesthood, a holy nation, God's own people, that you may declare the wonderful deeds of him who called you out of darkness into his marvellous light. Once you were no people but now you are God's people; once you had not received mercy but now you have received mercy.

1 Peter 2: 9–10

O Lord, who has taught us that all our doings without charity are nothing worth; Send thy Holy Ghost, and pour into our hearts that most excellent gift of charity, the very bond of peace and of all virtues, without which whosoever liveth is counted dead before thee: Grant this for thine only Son Jesus Christ's sake.

Collection for Quinquagesima, BCP

Almighty God, we beseech thee graciously to behold this thy family, for which our Lord Jesus Christ was contented to be betrayed, and given up into the hands of wicked men, and to suffer death upon the cross, who now liveth and

76

reigneth with thee and the Holy Ghost, ever one God, world without end.

Collect for Good Friday, BCP

Almighty and everlasting God, by whose Spirit the whole body of the Church is governed and sanctified; Receive our prayers which we offer before thee for all estates of men in thy holy Church, that every member of the same, in his vocation and ministry, may truly and godly serve thee; through our Lord and Saviour Jesus Christ. *Second Collect for Good Friday,* BCP

O Lord, we beseech thee, let thy continual pity cleanse and defend thy Church; and, because it cannot continue in safety without thy succour, preserve it evermore by thy help and goodness; through Jesus Christ our Lord.

Collect for Trinity 16, BCP

O Almighty God, who hast built thy Church upon the foundation of the Apostles and Prophets, Jesus Christ himself being the head corner-stone; Grant us so to be joined together in unity of spirit by their doctrine, that we may be made an holy temple acceptable unto thee; through Jesus Christ our Lord.

Collect for St Simon and St Jude, BCP

O Lord, without whom our labour is but lost, and with whom thy little ones go forth as the mighty; be present to all works in thy Church which are undertaken according to thy will (*especially . . .*) and grant to thy labourers a pure intention, patient faith, sufficient success upon earth and the bliss of serving thee in heaven; through Jesus Christ our Lord.

William Bright, 1824–1901

O God of unchangeable power and eternal light, look favourably on thy whole Church, that wonderful and sacred mystery; and by the tranquil operation of thy perpetual providence carry out the work of man's salvation; and let the whole world feel and see that things which were cast down are being raised up, and things which had grown old are being made new, and all things are returning to perfection through him from whom they took their origin, even Jesus Christ our Lord. Amen.

Gelasian Sacramentary

Prosper the labours of all Churches bearing the name of Christ and striving to further righteousness and faith in Him. Help us to place thy truth above our conception of it and joyfully to recognize the presence of thy Holy Spirit wherever he may choose to dwell among men. Teach us wherein we are sectarian in our intentions, and give us grace humbly to confess our fault to those whom in past days our Communion has driven from its fellowship by ecclesiastical tyranny, spiritual barrenness or moral inefficiency, that we may become worthy and competent to bind up in the Church the wounds of which we are guilty, and hasten the day when there shall be one fold under one Shepherd, Jesus Christ our Lord.

Bishop Brent of the USA, 1862–1929

O God, the Father of our Lord Jesus Christ, our only Saviour, the Prince of Peace; Give us grace seriously to lay to heart the great dangers we are in by our unhappy divisions. Take away all hatred and prejudice, and whatsoever else may hinder us from godly union and concord: that as there is but one Body and one Spirit, and one hope of our calling, one Lord, one faith, one baptism, one God and Father of us all, so we may henceforth be all of one heart and of one soul, united in one holy bond of truth and peace, of faith and charity, and may with one mind and one mouth glorify thee; through Jesus Christ our Lord.   *Accession Service, BCP*

To rule and govern your holy catholic Church; to guide all servants of your Church in the love of your word and in holiness of life; to put an end to all schisms and causes of offence to those who would believe; and to bring into the way of truth all who have gone astray:

R. *We implore you to hear us, good Lord*
                    Book of Lutheran Worship, USA

Ah, Lord God, thou holy lover of my soul, when thou comest into my soul, all that is within me shall rejoice. Thou art my glory and the exultation of my heart; thou art my hope and refuge in the day of my trouble. Set me free from all evil passions, and heal my heart of all inordinate affections; that being inwardly cured and thoroughly cleansed, I may be made fit to love, courageous to suffer, steady to persevere. Nothing is sweeter than love, nothing more courageous, nothing fuller nor better in heaven and earth; because love is born of God, and

cannot rest but in God, above all created things.
Let me love thee more than myself, nor love
myself but for thee; and in thee all that truly love
thee, as the law of love commandeth, shining
out from thyself.   Amen.

Thomas à Kempis, 1380–1471

O almighty God, who hast knit together thine
elect in one communion and fellowship, in the
mystical body of thy Son Christ our Lord; Grant
us grace so to follow thy blessed Saints in all
virtuous and godly living, that we may come to
those unspeakable joys, which thou hast prepared for them that unfeignedly love thee;
through Jesus Christ our Lord.

Book of Common Prayer

O God, who hast brought us near to an
innumerable company of angels and to the
spirits of just men made perfect; grant us in our
pilgrimage to abide in their fellowship, and in
our heavenly country to become partakers of
their joy; through Jesus Christ our Lord.

William Bright, 1824–1901

9

HOW OTHERS PRAY

9. HOW OTHERS PRAY

Lord of all creation, You have made us the masters of Your world, to tend it, to serve it, and to enjoy it. For six days we measure and we build, we count and carry the real and the imagined burdens of our task, the success we earn and the price we pay.

On this, the Sabbath day, give us rest.

For six days, if we are weary or bruised by the world, if we think ourselves giants or cause others pain, there is never a moment to pause, and know what we should really be.

On this, the Sabbath day, give us time.

For six days we are torn between our private greed and the urgent needs of others, between the foolish noises in our ears and the silent prayer of our soul.

On this, the Sabbath day, give us understanding and peace.

Help us, Lord, to carry these lessons, of rest and time, of understanding and peace, into the six days that lie ahead, to bless us in the working days of our lives.　Amen.　*Jewish Sabbath Prayer*

Now that evening has fallen,
To God, the Creator, I will turn in prayer,
Knowing that he will help me.
I know the Father will help me.

Dinka, Sudan

Ho! Great Spirit, Grandfather, you have made everything and are in everything. You sustain everything, guide everything, provide everything and protect everything because everything belongs to you. I am weak, poor and lowly, nevertheless help me to care in appreciation and gratitude to you and for everything. I love the stars, the sun and the moon and I thank you for our beautiful mother the earth whose many breasts nourish the fish, the fowls and the animals too. May I never deceive mother earth, may I never deceive other people, may I never deceive myself, and above all may I never deceive you. *Sioux Indian Prayer, Bishop Vine Deloria*

THE VOW OF THE BODHISSATVA

Living beings are without number: I vow to row them to the other shore. Defilements are without number: I vow to remove them from

myself. The teachings are immeasurable: I vow
to study and practise them. The way is very
long: I vow to arrive at the end.   *Buddhist*

ON A BIRTHDAY

Every passing year makes my life shorter and
time that is gone can never be recalled. Assist
me, Ahura Mazda, to be wise from the experi-
ences of the past and to move into the future
with joy and hope. Guide me to make the best
use of each day and each opportunity as they
come so that I may glorify the name of my
ancestors, my religion, my community and my
country. Grant me Thy clear and pure mind, I
pray, and devotion to Thee in everything I say
or do. May the heavenly sun light my way for
many a year to come and may Thy love and
blessings always be with me in life. May I always
remain worthy of Thy love!   *Zoroastrian*

FOR THE SPIRIT OF PRAYER

Help me, Ahura Mazda, to cultivate the habit of
prayer. Enable me to know Thy will. I pray that
I may conform my impulses to its demands. I

will pray with concentration of my mind and I
will pray with all my soul. I will pray to Thee in
words of devotion with all my heart and I will
pray to Thee aloud and I will pray to Thee in
silence, for Thou dost hear my prayers even in
thought. Thou dost read my thoughts and
measure my feelings and know my aspirations. I
will pray, Ahura Mazda, that prayer may lift me
to Thee and make me Thine.   *Zoroastrian*

PRAYER TO THE LIVING DEAD

O good and innocent dead, hear us: hear us, you
guiding, all-knowing ancestors, you are neither
blind nor deaf to this life we live: you did
yourselves once share it. Help us therefore for
the sake of our devotion, and for our good.

Mende, Sierra Leone

O God, I fear Thee not because
I dread the wrath to come: for how
can such affright, when never was
A Friend more excellent than Thou?

Thou knowest well the heart's design,
The secret purpose of the mind,
And I adore Thee, light divine,
Lest lesser lights should make me blind.

Muslim: Abū-l-Husain al-Nūrī

In the Name of God, the merciful Lord of
    mercy.
Praise be to God, the Lord of all being,
the merciful Lord of mercy,
Master of the day of judgement.
You alone we serve: to You alone we come for
    aid.
Guide us in the straight path,
the path of those whom You have blessed,
not of those against whom there is displeasure,
nor of those who go astray.

Muslim: Surah 1: The Fātihah, or Opener

Holy is God, the Father of all,
Holy is God, whose will is accomplished by his
    own powers,
Holy is God, who wills to be known and is
    known by his own,
Holy art thou, who by Logos has constituted all
    existing things,

Holy art thou, of whom all nature was born as
the image,

Holy art thou, whom nature has not formed,

Holy art thou, who art more mighty than all
power,

Holy art thou, who art greater than all emin-
ence,

Holy art thou, who art superior to all praises.

From the Hermetic Corpus,
a collection of prayers covering 1st to 3rd centuries AD

Open my eyes, O God, to behold true beauty,
divine beauty, pure and unalloyed, not clogged
with the pollutions of mortality and the vanities
of human life. So beholding beauty with the
eyes of the mind I shall be enabled to bring
forth, not images of beauty but realities, and
nourishing true virtue may become thy friend
and attain to immortality, O God of truth and
beauty.   *Based on a passage from Plato's* Symposium

May I be no man's enemy, and may I be the
friend of that which is eternal and abides. May I
never quarrel with those nearest to me; and if I
do, may I be reconciled quickly. May I never
devise evil against any man; if any devise evil
against me, may I escape uninjured and without

the need of hurting him. May I love, seek, and attain only that which is good. May I wish for all men's happiness and envy none. May I never rejoice in the ill-fortune of one who has wronged me . . . When I have done or said what is wrong, may I never wait for the rebuke of others, but always rebuke myself until I make amends . . . May I win no victory that harms either me or my opponent . . . May I reconcile friends who are wroth with one another. May I, to the extent of my power, give all needful help to my friends and to all who are in want. May I never fail a friend in danger. When visiting those in grief may I be able by gentle and healing words to soften their pain . . . May I respect myself . . . May I always keep tame that which rages within me . . . May I accustom myself to be gentle, and never be angry with people because of circumstances. May I never discuss who is wicked and what wicked things he has done, but know good men and follow in their footsteps.   *Eusebius, a late Ionic Platonist*

Now may every living thing, young or old, weak or strong, living near or far, known or un-known, living or departed or yet unborn, may every living thing be full of bliss.   *The Buddha*

How Others Pray

Day after day, O Lord of my life, shall I stand
      before thee face to face?
      With folded hands, O Lord of all worlds,
      shall I stand before thee face to face?
Under thy great sky in solitude and silence, with
      humble heart shall I stand before thee
      face to face?
In this laborious world of thine, tumultuous
      with toil and struggle, among hurrying
      crowds shall I stand before thee face to
      face?
And when my work shall be done in this world,
      O King of kings, alone and speechless
      shall I stand before thee face to face?

Rabindranath Tagore (1861–1941)

O Spirit of God, guide me
as I seek to discover thy working
with men of other faiths.
Give me the strength of truth,
the gentleness and strength of love,
the clear eye of judgement, and the courage of
   faith.
Above all, grant me a deeper understanding
of him who is the Truth,
a greater commitment to him who is the Lord,
a deeper gratitude to him

who is the Saviour of all,
even Jesus Christ thy Eternal Word,
through whom thou art drawing all men
to thyself, that they may be saved for ever,
and worship thee the only God
blessed for evermore.   *G.A.*

10

PRAYERS OF DEVOTION

10. PRAYERS OF DEVOTION

For thou lovest all the things that are,
    and abhorrest nothing which thou hast made:
    for never wouldest thou have made any thing
      if thou hadst hated it.
    And how could any thing have endured,
    if it had not been thy will?
    or been preserved, if not called by thee?
But thou sparest all: for they are thine,
    O Lord, thou lover of souls.

Wisdom 11: 24–6 (AV)

O God, I know that if I do not love thee with all
my heart, with all my mind, with all my soul and
with all my strength, I shall love something else
with all my heart and mind and soul and
strength. Grant that putting thee first in all my
lovings I may be liberated from all lesser loves
and loyalties, and have thee as my first love, my
chiefest good and my final joy.   *G.A.*

Drop thy still dews of quietness,
Till all our strivings cease;
Take from our souls the strain and stress,
And let our ordered lives confess
The beauty of thy peace.   *J. G. Whittier, 1807–92*

Prayers of Devotion

O thou who camest from above,
The pure celestial fire to impart,
Kindle a flame of sacred love
On the mean altar of my heart.

There let it for thy glory burn
With inextinguishable blaze,
And trembling to its source return
In humble prayer, and fervent praise.

Charles Wesley, 1707–88

O God, I am Mustafah the tailor and I work at
the shop of Muhammad Ali. The whole day long
I sit and pull the needle and the thread through
the cloth. O God, you are the needle and I am
the thread. I am attached to you and I follow
you. When the thread tries to slip away from the
needle it becomes tangled and must be cut so
that it can be put back in the right place. O God,
help me to follow you wherever you may lead
me. For I am really only Mustafah the tailor,
and I work at the shop of Muhammad Ali on the
great square.   *A Muslim's first prayer as a Christian*

Speak, Lord, for thy servant heareth. Grant us
ears to hear, eyes to see, wills to obey, hearts to
love; then declare what thou wilt, reveal what

thou wilt, command what thou wilt, demand what thou wilt—Amen.

Christina G. Rossetti, 1830–94

Grant to me, O Lord, to know what I ought to know, to love what I ought to love, to praise what delights Thee most, to value what is precious in thy sight, to hate what is offensive to Thee. Do not suffer me to judge according to the sight of my eyes, nor to pass sentence according to the hearing of the ears of ignorant men; but to discern with true judgement between things visible and spiritual, and above all things to enquire what is the good pleasure of thy will. *Thomas à Kempis, 1380–1471*

In times of doubts and questionings, when our belief is perplexed by new learning, new teaching, new thought, when our faith is strained by creeds, by doctrines, by mysteries beyond our understanding, give us the faithfulness of learners and the courage of believers in thee; give us boldness to examine and faith to trust all truth; patience and insight to master difficulties; stability to hold fast our tradition with enlightened interpretation to admit all fresh truth made known to us, and in times of

trouble, to grasp new knowledge readily and to combine it loyally and honestly with the old; alike from stubborn rejection of new revelations, and from hasty assurance that we are wiser than our fathers,
Save us and help us, we humbly beseech thee, O Lord.   *Bishop George Ridding, 1828–1904*

Father in heaven! When the thought of thee wakes in our hearts let it not awaken like a frightened bird that flies about in dismay, but like a child waking from its sleep with a heavenly smile.   *Søren Kierkegaard, 1813–55*

O God our Father, by whose mercy and might the world turns safely into darkness and returns again to light: We give into thy hands our unfinished task, our unsolved problems, and our unfulfilled hopes, knowing that only that which thou dost bless will prosper. To thy great love and protection we commit each other and all those we love knowing that thou alone art our sure defender, through Jesus Christ, our Lord.
The Church of South India

I have just hung up; why did he telephone?
I don't know . . . Oh! I get it . . .
I talked a lot and listened very little.

Forgive me, Lord, it was a monologue and not a
   dialogue.
I explained my idea and did not get his;
Since I didn't listen, I learned nothing,
Since I didn't listen, I didn't help,
Since I didn't listen, we didn't communicate.

Forgive me, Lord, for we were connected,
and now we are cut off.   *Michel Quoist*

Godhead in human guise
   Once to earth returning,
Daily through human eyes
   Joys of earth discerning:
Grant that we may treasure less
Passion than true tenderness,
   Yet never, Lord, despise
      Heart to sweetheart turning.
      Bless us, God of loving.

Jan Struther, 1901–53

O Blessed Jesu Christ, who didst bid all who
carry heavy burdens to come to thee, refresh us
with thy presence and thy power. Quiet our

understandings and give ease to our hearts, by
bringing us close to things infinite and eternal.
Open to us the mind of God, that in his light we
may see light. And crown thy choice of us to be
thy servants, by making us springs of strength
and joy to all whom we serve.

Evelyn Underhill, 1875–1941

Dear God, be good to me;
The sea is so wide,
And my boat is so small.　*Breton fishermen's prayer*

Day after day, O Lord of my life, shall I stand
　　　before thee face to face?
　　With folded hands, O Lord of all worlds,
　　　shall I stand before thee face to face?
Under thy great sky in solitude and silence, with
　　　humble heart shall I stand before thee
　　　face to face?
In this laborious world of thine, tumultuous
　　　with toil and struggle, among hurrying
　　　crowds shall I stand before thee face to
　　　face?
And when my work shall be done in this world,
　　　O King of kings, alone and speechless
　　　shall I stand before thee face to face?

Rabindranath Tagore (1861–1941)

O come, Holy Spirit, inflame my heart, set it on fire with love. Burn away my self-centredness so that I can love unselfishly. Breathe your life-giving breath into my soul so that I can live freely and joyously, unrestricted by self-consciousness, and may be ready to go wherever you may send me. Come like a gentle breeze and give me your still peace so that I may be quiet and know the wonder of your presence, and help diffuse it in the world. Never let me shut you out; never let me try to limit you to my capacity; act freely in me and through me, never leave me, O Lord and giver of life!

Michael Hollings and Etta Gullick

Thou wast transfigured upon the mountain, and thy disciples beheld thy glory, O Christ our God, as far as they were able to do so: that when they saw thee crucified, they might know that thy suffering was voluntary, and might proclaim unto the world that thou art truly the brightness of the Father.

Orthodox

FOR THE SPIRIT OF PRAYER

Help me, Ahura Mazda, to cultivate the habit of prayer. Enable me to know Thy will. I pray that

I may conform my impulses to its demands. I will pray with concentration of my mind and I will pray with all my soul. I will pray to Thee in words of devotion with all my heart and I will pray to Thee aloud and I will pray to Thee in silence, for Thou dost hear my prayers even in thought. Thou dost read my thoughts and measure my feelings and know my aspirations. I will pray, Ahura Mazda, that prayer may lift me to Thee and make me Thine.   *Zoroastrian*

O King enthroned on high,
Thou comforter divine,
Blest Spirit of all truth, be nigh
And make us thine.

Thou art the source of life,
Thou art our treasure-store;
Give us thy peace and end our strife
For evermore.

Descend, O heavenly Dove,
Abide with us alway;
And in the fullness of thy love
Cleanse us, we pray.   *8th century, tr. J. Brownlie*

O thou who camest from above,
The pure celestial fire to impart,

Kindle a flame of sacred love
On the mean altar of my heart.

There let it for thy glory burn
With inextinguishable blaze,
And trembling to its source return
In humble prayer, and fervent praise.

Charles Wesley, 1707–88

God give me work
Till my life shall end
And life
Till my work is done.

On the grave of Winifred Holtby, novelist,
1898–1935

II

THE BEYOND

11. THE BEYOND

O Father of all, we pray to thee for those whom we love, but see no longer. Grant them thy peace; let light perpetual shine upon them; and in thy loving wisdom and almighty power work in them the good purpose of thy perfect will; through Jesus Christ our Lord.

Book of Common Prayer (*1928*)

We give back, to you, O God, those whom you gave to us. You did not lose them when you gave them to us, and we do not lose them by their return to you. Your dear Son has taught us that life is eternal and love cannot die. So death is only an horizon, and an horizon is only the limit of our sight. Open our eyes to see more clearly, and draw us closer to you that we may know that we are nearer to our loved ones, who are with you. You have told us that you are preparing a place for us: prepare us also for that happy place, that where you are we may also be always, O dear Lord of life and death.

William Penn, 1644-1718

Father of all, I commend to thy mercy all my friends who have died, especially . . . Grant them more light and further opportunities for progress in the knowledge of thee. If it be possible, may they pray for me as I do now for them. Unite us in the communion of Saints and the fellowship of the Holy Spirit, for Jesus' sake.   *W. R. Matthews, 1881–1973*

PRAYER AT A FUNERAL

Today we stand before Thee, dear Ahura Mazda, with the earthly remains of . . . whom Thou hast called back to Thee. Nothing can bring warmth to this body. The light will never return to its eyes, the pulse will never throb anew and the heart will not resume its beating. None can breathe the breath of life back into it. It is now a lifeless piece of clay. The body is dead and the dead is dust.

Death has freed . . . from his material bondage. He has shed his frail earthly mansion and departed this life to live hereafter in the realm of the spirit. His earthly work is done and he has laid down his burden. From the din and dust of life's struggle, he has gone to the deathless world of peace and rest where light fades not and happiness fails not. Our beloved has died in body to live in spirit a life higher and nobler than our thoughts can measure and minds can conceive. Let him rest in everlasting peace and joy with Thee, Ahura Mazda.   *Zoroastrian*

O Lord, governor of heaven and earth, in whose hands are embodied and departed spirits, if thou hast ordained the souls of the dead to minister to the living, and appointed my departed wife to have care of me, grant that I may enjoy the good effects of her attention and ministration, whether exercised by appearance, impulses, dreams, or in any other manner agreeable to thy government; forgive my presumption, enlighten my ignorance, and however meaner agents are employed, grant me the blessed influences of thy Holy Spirit, through Jesus Christ our Lord.

Samuel Johnson, 1709–84

Eternity—the possession of all time, past, present, and to come, in full plenitude, in one single moment, here and now.

Boethius, 480–524

The Beyond

Rest eternal grant them
  After weary fight;
Shed on them the radiance
  Of thy heavenly light.
Lead them onward, upward,
  To the holy place,
Where thy Saints made perfect
  Gaze upon thy face.

English Hymnal, *No. 356, v. 4 (translated from Swahili)*

Go forth, Christian soul, from this world in the
name of God the Father almighty, who created
thee; in the name of Jesus Christ, the Son of the
living God, who suffered for thee; in the name
of the Holy Ghost, who was poured out upon
thee; in the name of the holy and glorious
Mother of God, the Virgin Mary; in the name of
blessed Joseph; in the name of angels and arch-
angels; in the name of thrones and dominations; in the name of principalities and powers;
in the name of cherubim and seraphim; in the
name of the patriarchs and prophets; in the
name of the holy apostles and evangelists; in
the name of the holy martyrs and confessors;
in the name of the holy monks and hermits; in
the name of the holy virgins and of all the saints
of God: today let thy place be in peace, and thine

abode in holy Sion. Through the same Christ
our Lord.   *Commendation of a soul, Western Rite*

There in that other world, what waits for me?
What shall I find after that new birth?
No stormy, tossing, frowning, smiling sea,
  But a new earth.

No sun to mark the changing of the days,
No slow, soft falling of the alternate night,
No morn, no stars, no light upon my ways,
  Only the light.

No gray cathedral, wide and wondrous fair,
That I may tread where all my fathers trod.
Nay, nay, my soul, no house of God is there,
  But only God!   *Mary Coleridge, 1861–1907*

And so all men, together everywhere,
and at all times, shall cry aloud to Thee
For joy of heart.
To whom be praise and worship, honour,
  strength.
A blessing and a song for evermore.

                              Alcuin, 725–804

12

FINAL BLESSINGS

12. FINAL BLESSINGS

With which to close, and await in silence with open and grateful hearts:

Unto God's gracious mercy and protection we commit you. The Lord bless you and keep you. The Lord make his face to shine upon you, and be gracious to you. The Lord lift his countenance upon you, and give you peace.

The Aaronic blessing, Numbers 6: 24–6

The God of peace, that brought again from the dead our Lord Jesus, that great shepherd of the sheep, through the blood of the everlasting covenant, make us perfect in every good work to do his will, working in us that which is well-pleasing in his sight; through Jesus Christ, to whom be glory for ever and ever.

Hebrews 13: 20, 21

May the Lord bless you with all good and keep you from all evil; may He give light to your heart with loving wisdom, and be gracious to you with eternal knowledge; may He lift up his loving countenance upon you for eternal peace.

Dead Sea Scrolls

Final Blessings

May God, the Lord, bless us with all heavenly benediction, and make us pure and holy in his sight.

May the riches of his glory abound in us.

May He instruct us with the word of truth, inform us with the Gospel of salvation, and enrich us with his love, Through Jesus Christ, our Lord. *Gelasian Sacramentary*

May the eternal God bless and keep us, guard our bodies, save our souls, direct our thoughts, and bring us safe to the heavenly country, our eternal home, where Father, Son and Holy Spirit ever reign, one God for ever and ever.

Sarum Breviary

May the road rise to meet you.
May the wind be always at your back.
May the sun shine warm upon your face.
May the rains fall softly upon your fields
    until we meet again
May God hold you in the hollow of his hand.

Old Gaelic blessing

May God in the plenitude of his love pour upon you the torrents of his grace, bless you and keep you in his holy fear, prepare you for a happy eternity, and receive you at last into immortal glory. *Blessing at the Consecration of Coventry Cathedral*

The blessing of the Lord rest and remain upon all his people, in every land, of every tongue; the Lord meet in mercy all that seek him; the Lord comfort all who suffer and mourn; the Lord hasten his coming, and give us, his people, the blessing of peace. *Bishop Handley Moule, 1841–1920*

Now may the God of peace who brought again from the dead our Lord Jesus, the great shepherd of the sheep, by the blood of the eternal covenant, equip you with everything good that you may do his will, working in you that which is pleasing in his sight, through Jesus Christ; to whom be glory for ever and ever. Amen. *Hebrews 13: 20–1*

Now to him who is able to keep you from falling and to present you without blemish before the presence of his glory with rejoicing, to the only God, our Saviour through Jesus Christ our Lord, be glory, majesty, dominion, and authority, before all time and now and for ever. Amen. *Jude: 24–5*

ACKNOWLEDGEMENTS
(Numbers refer to pages)

Quotations from the Scriptures are taken from either the Authorized King James Version of the Bible, the Revised Standard Version or the Revised Version.

Quotations from the Psalms are from the Book of Common Prayer 1662.

We are grateful for permission to include the following copyright material in this collection.

Extracts from the Revised Standard Version of the Bible, copyrighted 1946, 1952, © 1971, 1973 are used by permission of the National Council of the Churches of Christ.

George Appleton: © George Appleton. (34/5, 45, 63, 72/3)

George Appleton: 'O God of Goodness, in the mystery . . .' and 'O God, I know that if I do not love thee . . .' from *Jerusalem Prayers for the World Today* (66, 94); 'O Spirit of God, guide me' from *One Man's Prayers* (91/2). Used by permission of The Society for Promoting Christian Knowledge.

Authorized Daily Prayer Book (Jewish): Reprinted by permission of Singer's Prayer-Book Publication Committee. (11)

John Baillie: from *A Diary of Private Prayer* (1936). (23, 35/6, 63/4, 70)

from *Contemporary Prayers for Public Worship*, ed. Caryl Micklem. Reprinted by permission of SCM Press Ltd. (18)

Margaret Cropper: from *Draw Near*. Used by permission of The Society for Promoting Christian Knowledge. (31)

Dinka, Sudan: from *Prayers of African Religion* by Professor John Mbiti. Used by permission of The Society for Promoting Christian Knowledge. (85)

Monica Furlong: in *Dawn Through our Darkness*, ed. Giles Harcourt (Collins 1985). (72)

Dag Hammarskjöld: from *Markings*, trs. by Leif Sjoberg and W. H. Auden. Copyright © 1964 by Alfred A. Knopf Inc., and Faber & Faber Ltd. Used by permission. (58/9)

Gabrielle Hadingham: used by permission of The United Society for the Propagation of the Gospel. (64/5)

Michael Hollings and Etta Gullick: from *It's Me O Lord*. Reprinted by permission of the pub-

Acknowledgements

lisher, McCrimmon Publishing Co. Ltd., 10–12 High St., Great Wakering, Essex. (34, 40/41, 100)

Cecil Hunt: from *Uncommon Prayers*. First published 1948. Used by permission of Hodder & Stoughton Ltd. (37)

Martin Israel: from *The Pain that Heals*. Copyright © 1981 by Martin Israel and the Crossroad Publishing Company. Used by permission of Hodder & Stoughton Ltd. (64)

Jewish Day of Atonement: from *Forms of Prayer for Jewish Worship: Daily, Sabbath and Occasional Prayers* (1977). Used by permission of The Reform Synagogue of Great Britain. (25/6)

Jewish Sabbath Prayer: from *Forms of Prayer for Jewish Worship: Daily, Sabbath and Occasional Prayers* (1977). Used by permission of The Reform Synagogue of Great Britain. (84)

Julian of Norwich: from *Revelations of Divine Love*, ed. Dom Roger Hudleston OSB (Burns & Oates Ltd., 1952). Used by permission. (58)

Søren Kierkegaard: from *The Prayers of Kierkegaard* by P. F. Lefevre. Copyright 1956 The University of Chicago. Used with permission. (97)

Acknowledgements

Latin, 13th century: from 'S. Thomae Aquinatis' from *The Poems of Gerard Manley Hopkins* (4th edn., 1967), ed. W. H. Gardner and N. H. Mackenzie. © The Society of Jesus 1967. Reprinted by permission of Oxford University Press on behalf of The Society of Jesus. (46)

Liturgy of St James: from *The Alternative Service Book 1980*, © Central Board of Finance of the Church of England and reproduced with permission. (44)

W. R. Matthews: from *Seven Words*. First published 1933. Used by permission of Hodder & Stoughton Ltd. (105)

Mende, Sierra Leone: from *Prayers of African Religion* by Professor John Mbiti. Used by permission of The Society for Promoting Christian Knowledge. (97)

Eric Milner-White: from *My God My Glory* (10, 30, 33, 44/5); from *Procession of Passion Prayers* (34). Used by permission of The Society for Promoting Christian Knowledge.

Eric Milner-White and G. W. Briggs: from *Daily Prayer* (1941). Used by permission of Oxford University Press. (41)

Muslim: Surah I: from the Qur'ān translated by Kenneth Cragg. Used by permission. (88)

Acknowledgements

Orthodox: from *Festal Menaion: The Service Book of the Orthodox Church*, trans. by Mother Mary and Archimandrite Kallistos Ware. Used by permission of Faber & Faber Ltd. (100)

Prayer from Kenya: from *Morning, Noon and Night*, edited by the Revd. John Carden. Reprinted by permission of the Church Missionary Society. (37)

Prayer of a Nigerian Christian: from ibid. (22)

from *Prayers of African Religion* by Professor John Mbiti. Used by permission of The Society for Promoting Christian Knowledge. (72)

Michel Quoist: from *Prayers of Life*. Used by permission of the publishers, Gill & Macmillan Ltd., Dublin, and Andrews & McMeel Inc., USA. (98)

Yves Raquin, SJ: from *Paths to Contemplation*, translated by P. Barrett. Used by permission of Anthony Clarke Publishers. (9)

from *The Roman Missal*, © 1973 International Committee on English in the Liturgy, Inc., 2 offertory prayers (35, 45)

Sister Ruth, SLG: used by permission. (7/8, 35)

Léopold Sédar Senghor: 'Prayer for Peace',

117

Acknowledgements

Part V, Abridged, from *Selected Poems of Léopold Sédar Senghor*, trs. John Reed & Clive Wake. Copyright Editions du Seuil 1948. Translation © Oxford University Press 1964. Used by permission of Editions du Seuil, Georges Borchardt Inc., and Oxford University Press.

Jan Struther: extract from 'God, whose eternal mind . . .' from *Enlarged Songs of Praise*. Reprinted by permission of Oxford University Press. (98)

Rabindranath Tagore: from *Gitanjali*, in *Collected Poems and Plays*, copyright 1916 by Macmillan Publishing Co., Inc., renewed 1944 by Rabindranath Tagore. Used with permission. (27, 91, 99)

William Temple: from *Readings in St John's Gospel* (8, 30); from *The Prayer Manual* (ed. F. B. McNutt, 1951) (62/3) Reprinted by permission of Macmillan, London & Basingstoke.

Simone Weil: from *Waiting On God* (Collins/Fontana, 1981). (59)

Brian Wren: reprinted by permission of Oxford University Press. (47)

Acknowledgements

Zoroastrian: from *Let Us Pray to Ahura Mazda* by Noshir H. Vajifdar. Used with permission. (86, 87, 101, 105/6)